CHAPTER 1: INTRODUCTION TO TRANSFER LEARNING

Transfer learning is one of those game-changing ideas in the sphere of artificial intelligence: models performing one task are used doing a different one, capitalizing on knowledge acquired in the first task to improve performance in the second, especially key in AI communities, dealing with tasks including reduced labeled data. Basically, the idea is that you take a pre-trained modeland then fine-tune it on another, much smaller dataset that is related to a specific, particular task.

This does not only reduce the computational cost and time for the training of models from scratch, but it also performs better, in most cases, because rich, high-level feature representations were learned in the pre-training. As such, transfer learning is more akin to how humans leverage their acquired knowledge toward new problems, hence making this area a natural fit for creating AI systems: intelligent and adaptive.

For instance, a model trained to recognize objects in images on a large dataset, such as ImageNet, can be fine-tuned to recognize specific medical conditions in X-ray images using much fewer labeled examples. This adaptability is very useful in applications where data are either hard to come by or overly expensive to generate, such as in medical imaging, where there is a shortage of annotated datasets, though this is overcome by the availability of pre-trained models.

Even in applications related to image recognition, transfer learning spans natural language processing, speech recognition, and reinforcement learning. Transfer learning is a process that enables the knowledge transfer from one domain to another, as a result of which AI models are trained more efficiently and advanced technologies are made available for use in many other fields and industries.

Transfer learning also solves the overfitting problem, which occurs in a situation where a model undergoes fitting to a training dataset too well and, as a consequence, minimizes generalization on new, unseen data. In essence, transfer learning is the process of learning from a model that is pre-trained on some general features and patterns, with very little need for adjustment, and generalizes well.

This, therefore together, makes transfer learning an attractive means for the development of robust AI systems performing well across several scenarios and datasets. It is versatile and effective at the same time, which is why so much effort and innovation in AI development is going on in this era, leading to breakthroughs in areas that had previously been bound by constraints of data availability and computational resources.

CHAPTER 2: EVOLUTION OF TRANSFER LEARNING

The evolution path of transfer learning is spotted with some significant milestones and breakthroughs that took the approach from a theoretical concept to a practical tool applicable in a wide range of AI today. Transfer learning had traditionally been explored more when shallow machine learning algorithms dominated the field. The advent of deep learning technologies has opened up tremendous potential. In former attempts, transfer learning involved models that were pre-trained with a substantial amount of data for specific tasks, such as image classification, and these pre-trained models were applied against related tasks. With deep neural networks newly introduced, the approach gained new dimensions.

The seminal work on AlexNet—the winner of the ImageNet Large Scale Visual Recognition Challenge in 2012— showed the power of deep convolutional networks pre-trained on vast amounts of data. This was a watershed result in demonstrating how pre-trained models could produce state-of-the-art results with very little, if any, fine-tuning.

Next came VGG, followed by ResNet, then Inception: each of these beat the achievements of the previous ones and fine-tuned the same very process of transfer learning. Pretrained models learn hierarchical feature representation from gigantic volumes of data that can be transferred to most use cases—reducing the need for a large quantity of labeled data in the target domain.

Indeed, its ramifications are deep, extending far beyond the mere technical aspects of transfer learnings to altering the very milieu in which AI research and development take place. It's the democratization of access to any powerful pre-trained model that has put advanced AI techniques within reach of the smallest organization and the researcher, so often constrained by the current developed technology more than anything else.

This, in turn, brought forth a wave of creative applications and solutions in all these domains, from health and finance to agriculture and entertainment. The collaborative nature of transfer learning allows knowledge sharing and building on, which then provides fuel toward a more dynamic and open AI ecosystem, driving progress and innovation faster than ever.

CHAPTER 3: TYPES OF TRANSFER LEARNING

Transfer learning can be categorized in various types with respect to the connection related to source and target tasks and domains. Inductive transfer learning is guided by a labeled source dataset toward a labeled target task. This could be considered most useful and commonly used in practice. It is designed so that it improves the performance of the target task by transferring knowledge from the source task. For example, learning the everyday object recognition task can facilitate the recognition of many different classes of animals. This often means fine-tuning the pre-trained model on the new dataset, allowing it to learn details of the task domain but holding the knowledge it had learned during pre-training constant.

On the other hand, inductive transfer learning leverages the unlabeled target data at training time. The method trains a model on a source task and then transfers it to the target task by only transferring the learned information, without using the labeled target data. This kind of transfer learning becomes handy, especially when the target

Essentially, the model parameters are adjusted according to the structure and distribution of the target domain data, and further the generalization capability of the model toward achieving better performance on the target task. For example, a sentiment analysis model trained on a large corpus of movie reviews can be fine-tuned to analyze sentiments in social media posts, even when these latter tokens are unlabeled, through the understanding of the context and distribution of the new data.

The most important type is unsupervised transfer learning, in which both the source and target tasks are unsupervised. This refers to transfer from an unsupervised learning task in the source domain to another unsupervised task in the target domain. For instance, we may be doing something like applying a model trained on clusters of news articles to cluster scientific papers. Since no labeled data are available, the model still can utilize representations and patterns learned to conduct the target task well. These methods become useful in particular when obtaining labeled data is not feasible or is very costly.

Moreover, there is multi-task learning, which is transfer learning except that the model learns all the tasks simultaneously. This will help the model leverage shared representations and knowledge learned on different yet related tasks. By learning these tasks jointly, it can boost the performance of each single task with the shared information. For example, a model that is trained to detect objects and semantically segment images at the same time could use common features and patterns among these tasks and, therefore, do a better job overall.

CHAPTER 4: PRETRAINED MODELS AND THEIR FAMILIES

Pretrained models are the skeleton of transfer learning and constitute the skeleton on which to erect new structures or train experts. Such models are usually trained with vast datasets, acquiring a large number of general features and patterns relevant to a wide set of tasks.

One of the first highly influential pretrained models was AlexNet, which proved that deep convolutional neural networks are pretty effective for image classification. It was successful and helped pave the way forward for VGG with deeper networks but smaller convolutional filters and ResNet with residual connections that improved the vanishing gradient problem with even deeper networks.

All these models have a family with their strengths and innovations. It was with this family that inception modules were introduced, which allow the network to capture multi-scale features by using convolutions of different sizes within the same module. This innovation made the network enormously efficient and performant, making it suitable for a range of tasks. The DenseNet family focused on increasing information flow between layers by connecting every layer to all other layers in a feed-forward manner, thereby increasing parameter efficiency and leading to better gradient flow.

These families of pretrained models have made significant advances not just in image classification but also in those other cutting-edge domains, like natural language processing. Essentially, models like BERT, GPT, or their follow-up versions changed the game of NLP, recording the most complex relationships and the structure in text data encountered so far.

On the other hand, BERT uses a transformer architecture to learn bidirectional representations of sentences, so most NLP tasks can be done with high performance. In that regard, for example, GPT uses the generative approach to illustrate what the large-scale pretraining of models on text corpora can achieve for the purposes of generating coherent, contextually relevant text.

CHAPTER 5: APPLICATIONS OF TRANSFER LEARNING

Applications applicable for transfer learning are immense and cut across from one domain to another, ranging from industry to industry. In medical imaging, transfer learning has had a huge impact on medical imaging whereby models pre-trained on common image datasets have been fine-tuned to specific tasks, such as the detection of tumors or fractures in medical scans.

This approach is advantageous mainly because, say, diagnostic accuracy increases and the requirement of availability of a large amount of labeled medical data is reduced, which is generally scarce and very difficult to get at reasonable costs. Other applications of transfer learning have also been made in genomics, such as recognizing disease markers or predicting gene functions with models pretrained on genetic sequences.

Transfer learning has also recently revolutionized NLP, where it further pushed the state-of-the-art in tasks like machine translation, sentiment analysis, and text summarization. Particularly, these tasks have acquired new benchmarks by using models like BERT and GPT, which pose large-scale text corpora for learning more nuanced language representations. These models can further be fine-tuned toward any specific task with a very low quantity of labeled data required, hence proving really adaptive and effective. For instance, a pre-trained model for sentiment analysis on movie reviews can be fine-tuned for an e-commerce business value task involving customer feedback analysis.

Transfer learning has also been used in the automotive sector, particularly in the autonomity of automotive driving systems. The models pre-trained on extensive driving data could then be fine-tuned for utilization on varied or new driving conditions or surroundings, leading to better safety and reliability for autonomous vehicles

Similarly, in robotics, skills that could be learned through simulations can be transferred into robotic systems, enabling them to move on to real-world tasks much more cheaply and faster than one could have accomplished if they were to be trained from scratch. This has huge implications on manufacturing, healthcare, or any other sector where robots are fast being deployed.

CHAPTER 6: CHALLENGES AND LIMITATIONS

Apart from myriad benefits, transfer learning offers equal challenges and limitations. One of the major issues is negative transfer, which refers to the condition where the transferred knowledge from the source task deteriorates performance at the target task. This occurs most often if the source and target tasks are poorly relevant, and then the features and patterns learned are not in the right alignment.

Identification of the correct source tasks may be important to ensure at the same time that the source task bears the good level of similarity to the target task in order to minimize possible risks of negative transfer. The computational cost of fine-tuning large pre-trained models might be potentially high, which a resource-constrained organization might not afford.

Another weakness of transfer learning is the issue of bias in pretrained models. These models pick up biases mostly from the data they are trained on, often from data that is widely available on the internet. They learn and then further perpetuate this bias. This may include biased predictions and unfair outcomes, mainly regarding sensitive applications such as hiring and criminal justice.

These biases have to be dealt with via careful curation of training data and developing techniques that can mitigate bias in the learning process. Also, transfer learning models are still not very transparent, for the complex architecture and large number of parameters make it quite difficult to know how the models made their predictions.

Although transfer learning has shown a lot of promise in many domains, the effectiveness could differ from task to task and by dataset. Fine-tuning a pre-trained model is not always leading to dramatic improvements, in particular when the target task differs much from the source task. In this case, models shall be trained from scratch or domain-specific architectures shall be employed otherwise. Transfer learning has its pros and cons, so these things should be known explicitly and applied carefully for a particular application.

CHAPTER 7: FUTURE DIRECTIONS IN TRANSFER LEARNING

The future in transfer learning is promising, full of excitement and abounds in plenty of opportunities to better things. One of the more promising ways forward is in making transfer learning techniques more efficient and scalable. Because the sizes and complexities of pre-trained models continue to grow, methods that are least disruptive to computational cost and resource usage when fine-tuning such models are urgently needed. Other techniques that hold promise in this respect are knowledge distillation—training smaller models to mimic the behavior of larger models—and parameter-efficient transfer learning—fine-tuning only a subset of the model parameters.

Another very interesting line for future research is to focus on cross-modality transfer learning. Most of the applications of transfer learning that exist up to the present work for a single modality end, like images or text. This can, however, be made stronger and more flexible when combining information from several modalities, ranging from vision, language, and audio.

The underpinning drive to cross-modal transfer learning lies in leveraging the complementarity of the strengths exhibited by different modalities together to boost performances related to tasks that are evidently seen to be particularly challenging. For instance, fusion between visual and textual information gives rise to strengthened image captioning and visual question-answering, while that between audio and text gives rise to a strengthened speech recognition and synthesis.

Moreover, it is believed that transfer learning can benefit from recent advances in unsupervised and self-supervised learning. Quite literally, these methods aim to learn very useful representations from unlabeled data to later transfer to many different tasks. Given the large volumes of unlabeled data available, self-supervised methods stand poised to improve the effectiveness of transfer learning even further, particularly for domains in which labeled data is either scarce or simply does not exist.

However, techniques like contrastive learning, learning to differentiate between similar and dissimilar examples, or generative pretraining that generates new data samples are already leading to ever more powerful and flexible transfer-learning models.

CHAPTER 8: TRANSFER LEARNING IN NATURAL LANGUAGE PROCESSING

Transfer learning has already revolutionized the field of natural language processing, making huge strides possible in tasks such as language modeling, text classification, and machine translation. Perhaps the biggest line in transfer learning for NLP, though, is the development of models that are transformer-based.

While BERT represents a Bidirectional Encoder Representation from Transformers, GPT refers to a Generative Pre-trained Transformer, showcasing large-scale pretraining in diverse text corpora to learn rich language representations that could be fine-tuned for any particular task. For instance, BERT uses bidirectional processing to create a context from both the left and the right of a token, so its performance in question answering or named entity recognition tasks is really good.

Mindfulness means being present and aware of your thoughts and feelings toward money. This does not pertain only to the recognition of negative thoughts in your brain but also to the changing of them into positive thoughts. Mindfulness techniques like meditation and deep breathing help to minimize or reduce financial stress and anxiety.

The success of BERT and GPT model families has in its wake presented and spurred the creation of other variants of the transformer-based models, which normally try to outperform their predecessors based on their strengths. For example, the models RoBERTa (Robustly Optimized BERT Approach) and T5 (Text-to-Text Transfer Transformer) in a general way really pushed NLP transfer learning to new bounds. RoBERTa improves BERT by training on more data and longer sequences, while T5 consolidates a series of NLP tasks into a single framework and, hence, is illustrative of transfer learning capability. These models have established new state-of-the-art results across a broad spectrum of NLP tasks, underlining the strength of pre-trained language models.

CHAPTER 9: TRANSFER LEARNING IN COMPUTER VISION

Another area where transfer learning produced a sea change is in computer vision. The existence of very large-scale image corpora—such as ImageNet—has motivated increasingly better-performing pretraining strategies, which, in turn, can be adapted to a huge variety of vision tasks.

By the turn of the decade, models such as VGG, ResNet, and Inception already marked meetings with convolutional revolution, yielding strong feature representations useful for object detection, segmentation, and image classification tasks. These models have brought down the number of training hours and computational resources otherwise required to achieve state-of-the-art performance in many vision applications.

While there are many benefits of using out-of-the-box, pretrained models for computer vision tasks, their flexibility in terms of generalizing over different datasets and domains is strongest.

For instance, a model pretrained on ImageNet can be fine-tuned to perform tasks such as detection of tumors in medical images or classifying species in wildlife photographs. This variability is of great importance in fields where annotated labels are either extremely scarce or very costly to obtain.

Transfer learning allows one to fastly develop high-performance vision systems with maximum freedom for the scientist's or practitioner's innovation interests, while, at the same time, making use of all the anterior knowledge and representations embedded in these pretrained models.

CHAPTER 10: IMPLEMENTING TRANSFER LEARNING: PRACTICAL CONSIDERATIONS

All of these would have several practical considerations when implementing transfer learning right from selecting the right pre-trained model up to refining the same for the target task. The first step will be to select a model suitable for the requirement of the task. This is entirely subject to factors like the size of the dataset, similarity between the tasks for source and target, and the availability of the computational resource. For instance, models such as ResNet and DenseNet go well with tasks on image classification, while transformer-based models, such as BERT and GPT, work well for natural language processing applications.

After choosing the pre-trained model, the subsequent operation is the fine-tuning of the target data. To fine-tune a model means to adapt it to the particular features and idiosyncrasies of a target task. Typically, this consists of first freezing the lower layers of the model, which capture general features, and consequently training the higher layers. The latter are those focused on solving the task of interest. Finally, these layers can be gradually unfrozen and trained according to the complexity of the task at hand and data availability. The learning rate, batch size, and other hyperparameters should be well tuned in order to have the best performance possible and to be safe from overfitting.

Besides fine-tuning, data augmentation and regularization techniques may also be adopted as a course of action for better generalization and resiliency. Augmentation is a process in which a large corpus of generated examples, through rotation, scaling, and flipping operations, is used in the training in order to help the model learn invariant features and enhance performance on unseen data. Regularization aims to prevent overfitting by methods like dropout and weight decay and helps generalize well to new, unseen examples.

Finally, the evaluation of model performance after fine-tuning will be done. The measurement criteria—accuracy, precision, recall, F1 score—can still be used for the assessment of the model's effectiveness in finding the chances for enhancement.

Validating through all possible cross-validation techniques helps in the determination of the goodness of fit in subsets of data, thus broadening the generalization of the concept. It is very important that practitioners are able to leverage the full potential of transfer learning, so that the practical development of robust and high-performance AI systems can be possible.

CHAPTER 11 THE ROLE OF MODEL FAMILIES IN TRANSFER LEARNING

The breakthrough concept of model families was that it provided a modular manner by which the pre-trained models could be used to handle an arrangement of tasks. A model family simply refers to a group of models which are related in one respect that they share an architecture, but different in some other respects such that they could have been trained from various datasets or had some other varied configuration. These families, therefore, make very useful bases for transfer learning since they hold a lot of information from the respective training. There is, for example, the ResNet family. This model is very famous due to its very deep residual network. It has quite a number of versions: ResNet-50, ResNet-101, and ResNet-152, each having varying depth and complexity. It will then be flexible to choose a model that best fits the specific needs at hand in terms of performance and required computations.

It allows transfer learning to work so well because of the fact that model families can generalize across different tasks. Models pre-trained from these families capture rich feature hierarchies that can be useful for a wide range of applications. For example, besides being pretty simple and effective, the VGG family has been in wide use for image recognition tasks

Its different versions, like VGG-16 and VGG-19, have been trained on huge datasets; hence, making them a very good candidate for transfer learning where domains have limited data. These models allow to fine-tune and achieve a very high accuracy on target tasks at a minimum additional cost in terms of effort. This saves a lot of time and resources and also ensures that these models are well-optimized according to the application.

Model families, however, help in making this process of transfer learning much smoother by giving a consistent and highly standardized framework for experimentation and production. The existence of pre-trained models in such reputable model families ensures that researchers and developers can apply previously proven architectures and training methodologies with very high levels of trust. This consistency matters a great deal in practical applications where reproducibility and reliability are paramount.

For instance, the Inception family, with its innovative multi-path architecture, has had applications in a wide span of domains ranging from medical imaging to autonomous driving. All these success stories of models—across a variety of domains—bring out the urgency to exploit model families in transfer learning for robust performance that is reliable.

CHAPTER 12 FINE-TUNING PRE-TRAINED MODELS

Fine-tuning of pre-trained models is very important in this process of transfer learning to attain a certain task. This is where the pre-trained model on some large dataset gets its parameters adjusted to fit the new, smaller dataset of the target task. This fine-tuning is useful, particularly because it adapts rich feature representations learned from the pre-training, hence reducing data and computational resources for the target task. It is used in many applications today, particularly in image recognition and natural language processing tasks for attaining high accuracy with limited data.

Fine-tuning is generally initiated by selecting a pre-trained model related to the target task at hand. For example, if a model was trained using the ImageNet dataset, it would be useful for most image classification tasks due to the large number of varying visual features on which it was trained.

After selecting a pre-trained model, replace the final layers with task-specific layers. These new layers are then trained using the target dataset to teach the model about the specific features and fine points of the new task. In this phase, the earlier layers of the model, which hold general features, are often frozen to prevent them from updating, focusing learning on the new task-specific layers.

Fine-tuning also requires careful consideration of hyperparameters, such as the learning rate and batch size, to ensure optimal performance. The learning rate is generally quite small, so that large updates in the pre-trained weights can be avoided; thus, the model retains the learned experience in previous tasks while being fine-tuned for a new task. In addition, techniques such as data augmentation and regularization improve generalizability and avoid overfitting.

In addition, techniques such as data augmentation and regularization improve generalizability and avoid overfitting. There is always a balance to be achieved between retaining the valuable knowledge within the pre-trained model and being able to effectively adapt it in achieving high performance on any new task with limited data and resources.

CHAPTER 13: PRACTICAL APPLICATIONS OF TRANSFER LEARNING

The practical applications of transfer learning are huge and very diverse, including in industries and domains. Transfer learning has helped overcome the challenge of creating advanced diagnostic tools and medical imaging systems in the healthcare domain. Models pre-trained on large-scale image datasets have been fine-tuned to detect a specific condition, whether a tumor or a fracture, in X-ray and MRI images.

This method has massively contributed to increasing the accuracy and efficiency of medical diagnostics, thereby providing the possibility for early detection and treatment of diseases. It has also been applied in personalizing treatment plans and in predicting patient outcomes, attested by leveraging the pre-trained models for the analysis of patient data to identify those trends that carry meaning into clinical decision-making.

In natural language processing, transfer learning refactors the development of language models and text-based applications. Pre-trained models such as BERT, GPT, and T5 have been fine-tuned to several tasks like sentiment analysis, machine translation, and text summarization. These have made great successes in understanding and generating human languages, hence very useful tools for chatbots, virtual assistants, and content automation. Pre-trained language models can be fine-tuned to make complex systems in NLP using limited training data, greatly reducing time and money needed to develop such a system.

Transfer learning has also made huge strides in autonomous driving and robotics. Pre-trained models are applied to improve the perception and decision-making skills of an autonomous vehicle, enabling it to move in complex scenarios and make decisions immediately. For example, models pre-trained on big datasets of images including road scenarios and traffic situations are tuned to fine-tune or detect and recognize in real-time objects like pedestrians, vehicles, and traffic signs.

This procedure gives better accuracy and reliability to autonomous systems, resulting in much safer and more efficient systems. It has also applied transfer learning to the area of robotics, letting robots learn new tasks, where knowledge from some pre-trained models is leveraged to improve their adaptability and performance in varied applications.

CHAPTER 14 : TOP 20 MOST USED PRE-TRAINED MODELS IN TRANSFER LEARNING

Pre-trained models are one of the main improvements that have taken the transfer learning field forward. Those kind of models, typically built on extensive datasets with sophisticated architectures, has become a go-to tool to attack different tasks. Top 20 most used and highly regarded pre-trained models that are used are as follow:

BERT, short for Bidirectional Encoder Representations from Transformers, broke into the scene with the breakthrough capacity to understand context literally both ways: left-to-right and right-to-left. BERT has now become a foundational model for many NLP tasks, including text classification, question answering, and named entity recognition.

GPT-3: This third-generation generative pre-trained transformer is applied to tasks like text completion, translation, and even creative writing with the capability to generate language. In the process, it is set with millions of parameters to be able to generate contexts and human-like text.

T5, short for Text-To-Text Transfer Transformer, poses all NLP problems in the form of a text-to-text problem, which makes it extremely easy to apply to a great number of very different tasks— summarization or translation, for example. In this respect, it becomes extremely versatile and has many applications in store.

ResNet: Residual connections helped the ResNet to cross the vanishing gradient issue for deep networks. ResNet family stands as one of the most popular families used in problems related to image classification and object detection. For example, ResNet-50 and ResNet-101.

Inception: The speciality of the Inception model lies in the inception modules, and it was designed to handle the output size because of the receptive fields of different sizes. For instance, Inception v3 and Inception v4 are much applied in tasks such as image recognition.

EfficientNet: Rather, the uniqueness in the EfficientNet models lies in their contribution to balancing accuracy with computational efficiency through compound scaling. This way, they have better performance with fewer parameters in image classification tasks.

VGG: VGG is a general abbreviation for the Visual Geometry Group; in most cases, the models specifically named VGG-16 and VGG-19 come as simple or deep topologies. These models can always be applied in many image classification and feature extraction problems.

MobileNet: MobileNet models are focused on being mobile and embedded, yet efficient and low in computational cost, with reasonable accuracy. They are quite popular for real-time applications on mobile devices.

Xception: Xception is basically an extension of the Inception model. It uses depthwise separable convolutions and has been trending in performance and efficiency. These are used in tasks such as image classification and object detection.

DenseNet: This model is used in making features reused by allowing a dense connectivity between the feature layers—hence a decrease in the number of parameters. Applied in vision tasks, like segmentation and classification.

ALBERT: Lighter in weight, this version is shrunk from BERT but is on par in terms of speed of execution and performance. Applicated for NLP tasks to seek computational efficiency.

RoBERTa: A Robustly Optimized BERT Pretraining Approach: RoBERTa is based on BERT and goes a step ahead in training on an even larger dataset with longer sequences, improving performance on most NLP tasks.

DistilBERT: DistilBERT is a distilled version of BERT, small and efficient, yet retains most of the original performance.

BART (Bidirectional and Auto-Regressive Transformers): BART combines BERT and GPT, making it appropriate for text generation, summarization, and translation tasks.

Chapter 15: Practical Implementations of Top Pre-Trained Models

Applications of pre-trained models refer to the human translation and use of transfer learning power in practical actions to solve particular tasks at hand. In this section, we outline ways in which some of the top pre-trained models can be leveraged to solve problems across various domains, focusing on code snippets and strategies for implementing the same.

1. ResNet Image Classification

The main steps involved in using ResNet for image classification are as follows. First, a pre-trained ResNet model is loaded in famous deep learning libraries such as TensorFlow and PyTorch. Next, fine-tune the model according to your dataset.

```python
import torchvision.models as models
import torch
import torchvision.transforms as transforms
from PIL import Image
# Load pre-trained ResNet model
model = models.resnet50(pretrained=True)
model.eval()
# Define image transformation
preprocess = transforms.Compose([
    transforms.Resize(256),
    transforms.CenterCrop(224),
```

```
    transforms.ToTensor(),
    transforms.Normalize(mean=[0.485, 0.456, 0.406], std=[0.229, 0.224, 0.225]),
])
# Load and preprocess image
img = Image.open('path_to_image.jpg')
img_tensor = preprocess(img).unsqueeze(0)
# Make prediction
with torch.no_grad():
    output = model(img_tensor)
    _, predicted = torch.max(output, 1)
print('Predicted class:', predicted.item())
```

2. Text Classification with BERT

For text classification tasks, BERT can be fine-tuned on your dataset to achieve high performance. Here's a basic example using the Hugging Face `transformers` library:

```
```

```python
from transformers import BertTokenizer, BertForSequenceClassification, Trainer, TrainingArguments
from datasets import load_dataset

# Load pre-trained BERT model and tokenizer
model = BertForSequenceClassification.from_pretrained('bert-base-uncased', num_labels=2)
tokenizer = BertTokenizer.from_pretrained('bert-base-uncased')

# Load and preprocess dataset
dataset = load_dataset('imdb')
def tokenize_function(examples):
    return tokenizer(examples['text'], padding='max_length',
```

Bolster confidence by seeking and achieving small, incremental goals, reaching out for feedback, and celebrating every win. Get strong using achievement as fuel to take on those ever-so-important bigger challenges. Surround and immerse yourself with positive, supporting, and encouraging individuals who will always offer positive reinforcement.

```
    truncation=True)

tokenized_datasets = dataset.map(tokenize_function, batched=True)

# Define training arguments
training_args = TrainingArguments(
    output_dir='./results',
    evaluation_strategy='epoch',
    per_device_train_batch_size=8,
    per_device_eval_batch_size=8,
    num_train_epochs=3,
    weight_decay=0.01,
)

# Train the model
trainer = Trainer(
    model=model,
    args=training_args,
    train_dataset=tokenized_datasets['train'],
    eval_dataset=tokenized_datasets['test'],
)

trainer.train()
```

3. Object Detection with YOLO

YOLO models are used for real-time object detection. The following code snippet shows how to use a YOLOv5 model with the `yolov5` Python package:

```python
import torch

# Load pre-trained YOLOv5 model
model = torch.hub.load('ultralytics/yolov5', 'yolov5s', pretrained=True)

# Perform inference on an image
results = model('path_to_image.jpg')

# Print results and show image with bounding boxes
results.print()
results.show()
```

4. Image Segmentation with UNet

UNet is commonly used for medical image segmentation. Here's how you might implement it using TensorFlow and Keras:

```python
import tensorflow as tf
from tensorflow.keras.models import load_model

# Load pre-trained UNet model
model = load_model('path_to_unet_model.h5')
# Load and preprocess image
image = tf.keras.preprocessing.image.load_img('path_to_image.jpg', target_size=(256, 256))
image_array = tf.keras.preprocessing.image.img_to_array(image)
image_array = tf.expand_dims(image_array, axis=0) / 255.0
# Predict segmentation mask
mask = model.predict(image_array)
# Process and visualize mask
import matplotlib.pyplot as plt
plt.imshow(mask[0, :, :, 0], cmap='gray')
plt.show()
```

5. Language Generation with GPT-3

GPT-3 can generate human-like text based on prompts. OpenAI provides an API for this purpose. Here's a basic example using the OpenAI API:

```python
import openai
# Set up OpenAI API key
openai.api_key = 'your-api-key'
# Generate text using GPT-3
response = openai.Completion.create(
engine="text-davinci-003",
prompt="Once upon a time in a land far away",
max_tokens=100
)
print(response.choices[0].text.strip())
```

These practical implementations demonstrate how to leverage pre-trained models for various tasks, from image classification to text generation. By utilizing these models, practitioners can achieve high performance with reduced effort, making complex tasks more accessible
 and efficient.

www.ingramcontent.com/pod-product-compliance
Lightning Source LLC
Chambersburg PA
CBHW071946210526
45479CB00002B/831